Futhark

Table of Contents

Preface:	6
-Futhark Runes-	8
FEHU (Cattle)	10
ÜRUZ (AUROCHS)	12
THURISAZ (Thorn)	14
ANSUZ (Speech)	16
RAIDHO (Riding)	18
KENAZ (Torch)	20
GEBO (Gift)	22
WUNJO (Joy)	24
HAGL (Hail)	26
NAUTHIZ (Necessity)	28
ISA (Ice)	30
JERA (Year)	33
PERTHRO (Unknown)	35
ALGIZ (Life)	37
SOWILO (Sun)	39
TIWAZ (Tyr)	41
BERKANO	43
EHWAZ (Horse)	45
MANNAZ (Mankind)	47
Laguz (Water)	49

INGWAZ (Seed)	51
DAGAZ (Dawn)	53
OTHALA (Homeland)	55
Nordic Symbols	57
Valknut	58
Yggdrasil	60
Vegvisir	62
Triple Horn of Odin	64
Mjolnir	66
The Helm of Awe	68
Gallery	70

Preface:

Hello, my name is Brittany Nightshade and I've spent many years studying witchcraft and Pagan tradition. While on my journey I've did my best to keep a record of the rituals and anything Magickal I've learned along the way. I've used these notes to make my own Book of Shadows, my own Grimoire.

Due to popular demand I've taken the section on Runes from that book and put them into a compact handbook of their own for those who'd like to have something only pertaining to the Futhark Runes that they can place on their Altar, carry on their person or use as a quick reference guide.

I hope you find this simple handbook useful for whatever purposes you wish to use it for, whether it's meditation, spell crafting, study or just personal growth, I wish you luck on your journey.
 –Brittany Nightshade

-Futhark Runes-

These ruins can be directly applied to anything to imbue the magickal properties that the runes represent or used alongside spells to increase their rate of success and power.

These Sacred Sigils are great to incorporate into your own spells. They're also great to meditate upon and can unlock power that you previously didn't have access to. Use these runes in conjunction with the any spell to further enhance and add an element of self to your rituals.

Norse legend says that Odin hung from Yggdrasil, The World Tree, for nine days and nights, staring into the Well of Urd. He had pierced himself with his own spear to prove he was worthy of the knowledge that the Norns possessed. On the ninth night the runes revealed themselves to him and granted him all the knowledge they held. Odin's powers greatly multiplied making him one of the most powerful entities in the Cosmos.

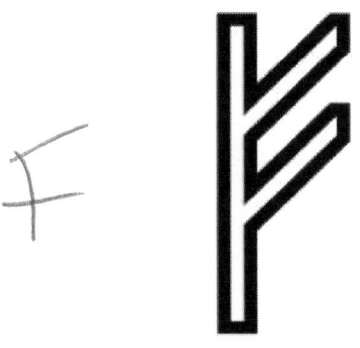

FEHU (Cattle)

Germanic: Fe (Fehu)
Gothic: Faihu
Norse: Fé
Anglo-Saxon: Feo, Feoh
Icelandic: Fé
Norwegian: Fe

Fehu literally translated means cattle, it is a symbol of wealth, property, and prosperity. This is the rune of luck and as such dictates the capacity to harbor luck and make use of it.

Fehu has the power to bless new endeavors and assist in making new goals. While being a rune of wealth, the fact that it is also directly tied to luck suggests that an altruistic nature is required to make us of its power, as luck is a result of courageous deeds.

This is a useful rune to use when performing rituals related to wealth, luck, love, and prosperity.

Stones associated with this rune are Tiger Eye, Carnelian, Citrine, and Aventurine.

ÜRUZ (AUROCHS)

Anglo-Saxon: UR
Germanic: Uraz (Uruz)
Gothic: Urus
Norse: Úr
Anglo-Saxon: Ur
Icelandic: Úr
Norwegian: Ur

Aurochs are a species of wild ox that lived in the European forests until it was hunted to extinction in the 1600's. This rune is the cosmic seed, beginnings and origins. It is masculine in nature and gives strength, endurance and athleticism. It is a rune of courage and boldness, freedom, rebellion, and independence. Ur represents the horn or the erect phallus, resurrection, life after death. Coming, being and passing away.

Represents the transfer of energies, used for projecting or drawing in of energy. Repeated use of the rune will gradually increase the amounts of energy one can handle at any given time. Helps in the growth of one's own reserves of power.

Stones associated with this rune are Agate, Epidote, Fire Agate, Diamond.

THURISAZ (Thorn)

Germanic: Thyth (Thurisaz)
Gothic: Thauris
Norse: Þurs
Anglo-Saxon: þorn
Icelandic: Þurs **Norwegian:** Thurs

Thurisaz represents the Jotnar (giants) and is the Rune of Power, Pain, Sharpness and Cutting. Thurisaz is derived from the words twer/tur which means to twirl, rotate, swirl or move. This is a destructive ruin of Chaos and Power. Use this rune to break down barriers, destroy, transform and create. Chaos is the true nature of this rune and a strong will and mind is needed to control it. This rune can be used in conjunction with other runes and spells for manifestation purposes.

The Rune itself is constructed in a way to represent a thorn.

This rune is very effective when used with a bloodstone. Using this rune with hematite can be very effective in deflecting curses. Use a pointed crystal to help project the energy of this rune.

Stones associated with this Rune are Bloodstone, Hematite, Cloudy Quartz, Agate, and Malachite.

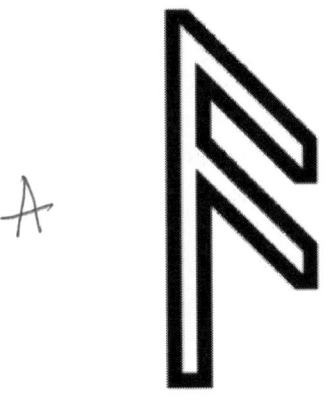

ANSUZ (Speech)

Germanic: Aza (Ansuz)
Gothic: Ansus
Norse: Óss, Áss
Anglo-Saxon: Aesc, (Os, Ac)
Icelandic: Óss, Áss

Ansuz is a rune that refers to speech and communication, the word Ansuz is thought to mean mouth which is meant to infer speech. The rune represents Odin, The All-Father, and is a rune of consciousness, mysticism, and mind.

Opens channels of self-expression and overcomes obstacles of every kind. Used in initiating oneself with Odin and assists in enhancing one's psychic and magickal abilities.

Ansuz also serves as a representation of breath, which can refer to the spirit. This Rune is capable of evoking inspiration and is commonly used by artists and students of the occult. This Rune has been found on many ancient artifacts, mainly staffs and rings.

Stones associated with this Rune are Lapis Lazuli, Moldavite, Opal, and Kyanite.

RAIDHO (Riding)

Germanic: Reda (Raidho)
Gothic: Raida
Norse: Reið, Reiðr
Anglo-Saxon: Rad
Icelandic: Reið
Norwegian: Reid, Reidr

Raidho refers to travel, motion, and journeys. This rune is used to reveal the best way to proceed in a given situation and is able to illuminate the best path to take in our lives.

In German Rad means wheel, which is where this rune derives its name from and is also where the words road and ride come from. Also, the Icelandic word for advice is Rada and from these two meanings we can surmise what this rune represents.

The construction of this rune is a combination of the Isa and an inverted Sowilo rune. The Zig Zag shape represents a journey that changes directions moving downward along the staff of the rune.

Like Ansuz, Raidho is a rune representing Odin, who was known as The Wanderer and The Rider. It is a rune of travel, journeys, and physical endurance, all of which Odin was known for. This rune has been used as a charm for travelers and as a guide for the dead in their journey to the afterlife.

Stones associated with this rune are Opal, Quartz, Lolite (water sapphire), Ametrine, Dendritic Agate and Kyanite.

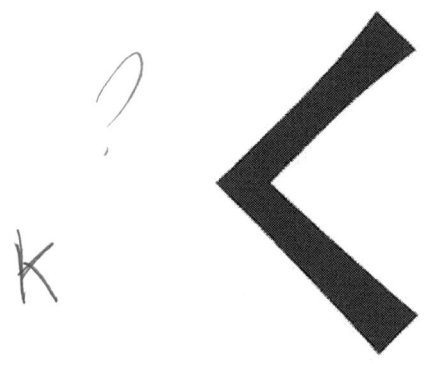

KENAZ (Torch)

Germanic: Chozma (Kenaz)
Gothic: Kaun
Norse: Kaun
Anglo-Saxon: Cen, Ken
Icelandic: Kaun
Norwegian: Kaun

Rune of light. The light of the soul and intellect. The traveler on the road to the underworld carried Kaun to illuminate and guide. The construction of this rune is of a delta for smooth flight and penetration.

The origin of the word is thought to be from the German Kennen, which means to know.

This rune also represents ulcers, sores, inflammations, swelling and boils and can be used in magick dealing with such.

This rune can be used in meditation to achieve enlightenment and esoteric knowledge.

Stones associated with this rune are Fire Agate, Fire Opal, Citrine, Garnet, Ruby Sun Stone and Amber.

GEBO (Gift)

Germanic: Geuua (Gebo) Gothic Giba
Norse: Gipt, Giöf
Anglo-Saxon: Geofu (Gyfu)
Icelandic: Gjöf
Norwegian: Giof

Gebo is a rune of sacrifice and giving. Something of personal value given freely, such as our blood when we choose to consecrate the runes in this way. This is a rune of initiation where we make personal sacrifices to obtain knowledge, power and wisdom such as when Odin hung from Yggdrasil for 9 days to attain knowledge.

Gebo is commonly used in Sex Magick and wedding rituals as it is deeply tied to the exchange of sexual energies between partners.

Stones associated with this rune are Emerald and Jade. Used with the Isa rune, the combination is powerful in binding enemies.

WUNJO (Joy)

Germanic: Uuinne (Wunjo)
Gothic: Winja
Norse: Vend
Anglo-Saxon: Wynn
Icelandic: Vin
Norwegian: Wynn

Wunjo is the rune of joy, used to bind us with those we care for and for strengthening those bonds. It is a rune of harmony, friendship, community and family. Wunjo has the ability with banishing the hurdles that keep us from bonding and foment alienation. Use Wunjo as a Ward to prevent the sorrows that would keep you from achieving your maximum level of consciousness. Community is the embodiment of this rune and all the things that make-up that community; love, trust, health, and divine will.

Wunjo is commonly known as the rune of perfection and correct wishing. We can utilize the power of Wunjo to marry our dreams to our actions to achieve our maximum potential.

Stones associated with this rune are Topaz and Clear Quartz.

HAGALAZ (Hail)

Germanic: Haal (Hagalaz) Gothic Hagl
Norse: Hagall
Anglo-Saxon: Hægl
Icelandic: Hagall
Norwegian: Hagall, Hagl

This rune represents hailstones. Involuntary sacrifice with no reward; a rune of suffering and injustice. A rune of destruction, disaster and catastrophe.

This rune is often used in black magic, sending destruction in the form of whatever runes are used with it, delivering violent loss and pain.

While this rune is typically used for harmful reasons it can also be used to gain understanding of what we cannot control. It symbolizes fate and can be used to gain insight into our divine nature and the will of the gods. Use this rune in conjunction with other runes to discover what fate has in store for you or others regarding specific areas of life.

For example, you can gain insight on the outcome of family ordeals by pairing this rune with Wunjo. Whereas you can attempt to alter fates by pairing this rune with Nauthiz and communing with the Norns who control the fates of humanity.

Stones associated with this rune are Ruby, Aquamarine, Onyx and Cassiterite.

NAUTHIZ (Necessity)

Germanic name: Noicz (Nauthiz)
Norse name: Nauð, Nauðr
Anglo-Saxon name: Nied (Nyd)
Icelandic name: Nauð
Norwegian name: Naudr, Naud

Nauthiz is a rune of endurance, will, and the mental strength needed to last. It represents the dark night of the soul and is connected to the Hagl rune.

Nauthiz can be utilized to realize what we need in spite of what we desire. It has the ability to empower us with the wisdom to see what must be done in an otherwise difficult situation.

When used in white magick, this rune gives defiance and the strength to carry on when all hope seems lost. It is a rune of survival and fearlessness in the face of death. When directed at another, this rune can give the spiritual strength to carry on and endure in the face of disaster.

Stones associated with this rune are Obsidian, Apatite, Carnelian and Azurite.

ISA (Ice)

Germanic: Icz (Isa)
Gothic Eis
Norse: Íss
Anglo-Saxon: Is
Icelandic: Íss
Norwegian: Is

Isa is a rune of binding. It represents stealth and is used in operations where one wishes to proceed undetected from spiritual or physical entities.

In nature, ice creeps up on the land, quietly freezing and immobilizing everything in its path while unaware fall victim to it. Isa is a rune of binding and preventing action through hidden means. It can halt a plan and prevent something from developing. It is used to conceal and can render a victim unaware of impending personal disaster to where any actions attempted will be too late in coming.

It is also used in preventing any action from a known hostile party. Isa freezes action and is the rune of cold, barren stillness, and death. Isa is the polar opposite of Fehu, as Fehu is a rune of movement and Isa is a rune of binding.

This rune is helpful in meditation as it acts to still the mind and help concentration, bringing calmness and guidance. Care needs to be taken as the rune can also make the user dull and/or obsessive. Isa works to calm hysteria, hyperactivity and restlessness. Often used in revenge spells and defense, it helps focus the will of the operator. Used with other runes, it acts to bind and shield the energies and keep them from interacting with each other.

Stones associated with this rune are Malachite, Obsidian, Smoky Quartz, and Diamond.

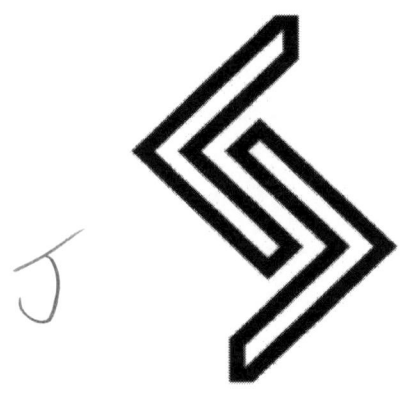

JERA (Year)

Germanic name: Gaar (Jera)
Gothic: Jer
Norse: Ár
Anglo-Saxon: Ger (Jara)
Icelandic: Ár
Norwegian: Jara, Ar

Jera is a rune of cycles and is symbolic of the harvest where the efforts of planting and work in the fields are rewarded with crops. Ar represents the cycles of change. Life cycles, lunar cycles, the cycles of the seasons and changes.

Jera is in contrast to Isa where everything stops, it signifies the return of the Sun and brings action. Ar symbolizes a vortex of cycling energy; the eight-fold wheel of life, the point inside of the circle, which is the glyph for the Sun meaning regeneration.

Ar can bring a reversal of personal fortunes. Like the Tarot Card, the Wheel of Fortune, Ar can reverse circumstances so misfortune is replaced with luck and visa-versa.

Rune of patience and awareness, moving in harmony with natural cycles. This rune is excellent for working with nature and is a rune of fruitfulness.

Ingwaz is the seed planted, Berkano is the earth that receives it and Jera is the growth and the harvest. A rune of long-term planning and persistence that helps ensure the success of plans.

Stones associated with this rune are Moss Agate, Lepidolite, and Moonstone.

EIHWAZ (Yew Tree)

Germanic name: Ezck (Eihwaz)
Gothic: Eihwas
Norse: Elhaz
Anglo-Saxon: Yr (Ēoh)
Norwegian: Eo

The Eihwaz rune represents the yew, the tree of life and death. This rune is frequently compared to the death tarot and holds many of the same meanings. Eihwaz is a rune of transformation, the death and beginning of something new.

This rune can represent the reversal of a current situation, or the beginning of something new coming from the ashes of old habits or attachments. Eihwaz is designed in a way to show the duality that is life and death and their inseparable connection.

Eihwaz reminds us to not fear death, it is merely a part in the cycle of life and rebirth and should be welcome as it heralds in change and new beginnings.

Stones associated with this rune are Aquamarine, Gold stones, and Chrysocolla

PERTHRO (Unknown)

Germanic name: Pertra (Perthro)
Gothic: Pairthra
Norse: Perð
Anglo-Saxon: Peordh (Pertra)
Icelandic: Perð, (Plástur)
Norwegian: (Pertra)

Perthro is a rune of divination. The unknown represents our fate and the impact one has on their lives. Our fates are tied to our actions and luck and with divination we have the ability to ask The Norns to give us a glimpse into what may be if we remain on our current course.

Perthro is the most mysterious of runes as it deals with the mysteries of the other runes and life itself and our relationship with them. Fate, Chance, and Action are undeniably linked creating a web between ourselves, the gods, and the universe. This rune ultimately represents these links and can be used for divination purposes in conjunction with other runes or by itself to ask favor and insight from the Spinners of Fate.

Stones associated with this rune are Onyx, Amethyst, Labradorite, and Sapphire.

ALGIZ (Life)

Germanic name: Algis, Algiz or Elhaz
Gothic: Algs
Anglo-Saxon name: Eolh
Norwegian name: Elgr

Algiz is the rune of life, it is constructed in a way as to represent 3 branches atop the World Pillar. Symbolic of a tree reaching up towards the heavens.

Algiz is a powerful rune of protection and represents the greatest defense that exists in the futhark runes. The 3 branches also represent the horns of an elk which are able to attack as well as defend.

This rune should be used as a shield against spiritual and physical attacks. It represents the power of man and the divine fate to uphold the order created by the gods in defense of Asgard and Midgard.

It is also used in consecration and the banishing of negative energies. It is excellent for witches to wear when performing dangerous rituals as it protects against negative energies, it can also be carved into an object and placed upon an altar or spell-space.

Stones related to this rune are Amethyst, Emerald, Fire Agate, Yellow Jasper, Smoky Quartz, Kunzite, Labradorite and Obsidian.

SOWILO (Sun)

Germanic: Sugil (Sowilo)
Gothic: Sauil
Norse: Sól
Anglo-Saxon: Sigel
Icelandic: Sól
Norwegian: Sol Old
Danish: Sulu
Old German: Sil, Sigo, Sulhil

The rune of the Sun and the counterforce to Isa, the rune of Ice.

Sowilo is a rune of action, honor, invincibility, and final triumph. A rune of movement that bestows the will to take action. It symbolizes the chakras/hvel and the lightning bolt, the spark of life.

It has both shielding and combative properties.

Used in understanding the energy forces in the world and on the astral. When used with other runes, it activates and empowers them. It can be used in meditation and to empower the chakras.

Brings out one's leadership abilities and one's ability to inspire others. Enhances one's strength of spirit.

Stones associated with this gem are Ruby, Red Spinel, Red Garnet, Rubellite, and Diamond.

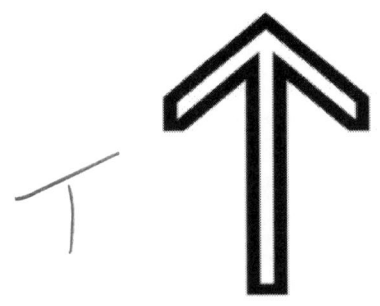

TIWAZ (Tyr)

Germanic: Tys (Tiwaz)
Gothic: Teiws
Norse: Týr
Anglo-Saxon: Tir, Tiw
Icelandic: Týr
Norwegian: Ty

The Tiwaz rune is associated with Tyr, the sky god of justice.

The rune is constructed in a way to represent a balanced spear-point which indicated movement in a single or upward direction. This rune also represents sacrifice as Tyr sacrificed his hand to bind the wolf of chaos Fenrir.

Tiwaz is a rune of harmony, justice, and the warrior. It represents honor which is representative of the sacrifice Tyr made to uphold the cosmic order.

Used for stability and the binding of chaotic energies. Good for defense and revenge workings as it represents justice.

Stones associated with this rune are Hematite, Sunstone, Bloodstone, Tiger Eye, and Heliotrope

BERKANO (Birch Goddess)

Germanic: Bercna (Berkano)
Gothic: Bairkan
Norse: Bjarkan
Anglo-Saxon: Beroc
Icelandic: Bjarkan
Norwegian: Bjarkan

Berkano is a rune that gets its name from the Birch tree which represents regeneration and youth. The rune alludes to the female form and is constructed to represent the breasts of a woman or the belly of a pregnant woman.

Berkano represents birth and rebirth after destruction. It is commonly associated with the goddess Ostara, goddess of spring and rebirth.

This rune can be used in workings for female fertility, feminine magick, and nurturing. It is used in concealment and protection.

This rune symbolizes feminine energies. It is an old Pagan custom to enclose a child at birth with the protective energies of Berkano, which remain with them throughout their lives.

Stones associated with this rune are Rose Quartz, Garnet, Agate, and Clear Quartz

EHWAZ (Horse)

Germanic: Eys (Ehwaz)
Gothic: Aihwa
Norse: Ehol, Ior
Anglo-Saxon: Eoh
Icelandic: Eykur
Norwegian: Eh, Eol

Represents the horse and is constructed in a way to appear as two horses facing one another, an allusion to the horses Árvakr and Alsviðr pulling the chariot of the Sun. It is also closely identified with Castor and Pollux the Gemini twins.

Ehwaz represents duality and the female and male aspects. Used to see into the future and for psychic communication.

Like the fourth chakra, this rune unites opposites. This rune forges bonds and is used to seal marriages and friendships.

Used in spiritual divination to understand the will of the Gods. Used to empower thought forms and bring them under the control and will of the mage. When used with other runes, Eihwaz unites the energies harmoniously.

Stones that are associated with this rune are Agate, Chrysoprase, Citrine, Moonstone, Pear, and White Sapphire.

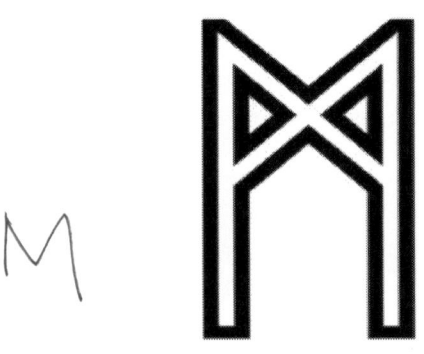

MANNAZ (Mankind)

Germanic: Manna (Mannaz)
Gothic: Manna
Norse: Maðr
Anglo-Saxon: Mann
Icelandic: Maður
Norwegian: Madr

Mannaz represents the link between mankind and the gods. Mannaz has a type of twisting in its structure representing how the fate of mankind and the gods are intertwined and cannot be undone.

The shape of the rune is two Wunjo runes facing one another, one representing man and the other the gods.

The Mannaz rune can be used in prophetic magick, can also be used to commune with the gods.

This rune is a rune of destiny and fate and can be used to improve oneself and can be used in any ritual that involves asking for help from the gods.

Stones that are associated with this rune are Sapphire, Celestite, Agate, Moonstone, and Tiger's Eye.

Laguz (Water)

Germanic: Laaz (Laguz)
Gothic: Lagus
Norse: Lögr
Anglo-Saxon: Lagu
Icelandic: Lögur
Norwegian: Laukr

Laguz is a rune that is meant to symbolize the downward flowing water that is full of energy. It also represents the concept of quantity as opposed to quality. The downward slope in the rune represents water flowing downhill.

Laguz also represents unbridled chaotic energy and the erosive forces of nature.

Can be used in rituals dealing with releasing control over a situation, this can be useful in stress reduction magick.

Stones associated with this rune are Lapis Lazuli, Azurite, Amethyst, Aquamarine and Sapphire.

INGWAZ (Seed)

Norse: Ing, Ingvarr
Gothic: Iggws
Germanic: Enguz (Ingwaz)
Anglo-Saxon: Ing
Icelandic: Ing
Norwegian: Ing

Ingwaz is a rune of isolation used for preparing a space for new growth to begin. It is the rune of gestation and internal growth. It represents the ancient image of God, Ing, and is a rune of male fertility.

Creative action, stored energy, power from meditation are all good examples of Ing, it is a rune of action and everything needed to

perform that action. The idea of sacrifice is a core component of Ingwaz, for something new to come about there must be something that is let go, an internal or external change must occur.

One of the main reasons a spell or ritual might fail is the inability of the practitioner to make the necessary sacrifices to achieve their goals and Ingwaz can help us understand what this might be. Use this rune as part of a pre-casting meditation ritual.

Stones associated with this Rune are Zircon, Peridot, Prehnite, and Tanzanite.

DAGAZ (Dawn)

Germanic: Daaz (Dagaz)
Gothic: Dags
Norse: Dagr
Anglo-Saxon: Daeg
Icelandic: Dagur
Norwegian: Dagr

The counterpart to the Jera Rune. Dagaz represents the daily cycle as Jera represents yearly and both are runes of change. Dagaz is the rune of spiritual awakening and is a symbol of light. The construction of the rune is that of an infinity symbol or an overturned hourglass, representing timelessness and limitless potential.

This rune is used to to attain inspiration and enlightenment. Meditate with this rune to discover the answer to a problem you've been facing. As its name entails Dagaz is able to shine light on an otherwise ambiguous situation and can be useful in any ritual involving answers and understanding.

Stones associated with this rune are Lapis Lazuli, Moonstone, Sunstone, Ruby, and Jade.

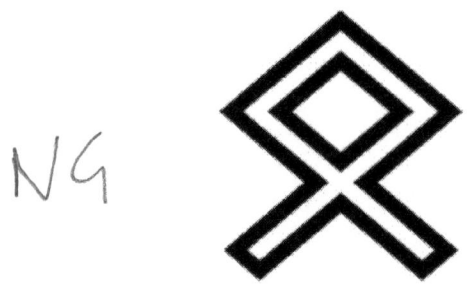

OTHALA (Homeland)

Germanic: Utal (Othala)
Gothic: Othal
Norse: Oðal
Anglo-Saxon: Otael (Ethel)
Icelandic: Óðal
Norwegian: Ödal

Othala governs any matter dealing with ancestry, inheritance, family and estate. Similar to Fehu it is a rune of Wealth and property but as Fehu represents the beginnings of wealth and its transformation over time Othala represents the immovable wealth that has been generated by your ancestral line.

This rune governs all aspect of inheritance whether it be material wealth, such as land, or talents passed down from your parents and even your genetic makeup.

Stones associated with this rune are Moss Agate, Pyrite, Citrine, and Garnet.

This rune governs all aspect of inheritance whether it be material wealth, such as land, or talents passed down from your parents and even your genetic makeup.

Stones associated with this rune are Moss Agate, Pyrite, Citrine, and Garnet.

Nordic Symbols

In addition to the Futhark Runes the ancient Nordic people made use of many symbols that hold similar esoteric power.

You can use these symbols in the same way as the runes, they can be incorporated into spells and rituals, engraved onto an object or even tattooed to imbue their magickal properties. In this section I'll be going over a few of the more well-known and used Nordic symbols; their meanings and their origins.

Valknut

The Valknut, pronounced "VAL-knoot" is a symbol of Odin. The root words that make up Valknut are Valr, meaning Slain Warrior and Knut, meaning knot. Therefore, the meaning of Valknut would be Knot of the Slain Warrior.

The 9 corners of the 3 interlocking triangles represent the 9 worlds and the cycle of life and death. Some believe the knot-like nature of the design to be symbolic of Odin's ability to bind or unbind the minds of warriors, to instill bravery and extinguish fear.

The Valknut is commonly found in burial sites of fallen warriors and who died valiantly in battle, this symbolized their courage and suggested they would join Odin in Valhalla to feast and battle with one another until the day they'd join with the gods to fight against impending doom during Ragnarök.

In summary the symbol of The Valknut represents destiny, bravery, courage and the cycle of life and death.

Yggdrasil

One of the most common and well-known Nordic symbols is the tree of life, Yggdrasil. Yggdrasil, pronounced "IHG-drah-sell", is a legendary ash tree that connects the nine worlds/realms to one another.

The world tree isn't inclusive to Nordic faiths

and is found in many religions around the world where it commonly represents the interconnectedness of all things and the cyclical nature of existence.

Yggdrasil is the tree that Odin himself hung upon during his quest for wisdom. The death-dragon Nidhogg chews at its roots to attempt to bring Chaos to the realms and the eagle of discord nests atop its branches. Ratatoskr the squirrel travels back and forth delivering messages enticing these monsters to destroy the tree to bring about the eventual change and rebirth that Yggdrasil represents.

Yggdrasil represents life and its interconnectedness, but most importantly the fact that life is ever changing and in a constant cycle of life, death, and rebirth.

Vegvisir

The Vegvisir, pronounced "VEGG-vee-seer", is a Runic Compass and is believed to provide guidance to those who have lost their way. It is believed that this symbol might have been drawn on Viking ships before an expedition to ensure that they'd be able to find their way home.

Icelandic lore says that one who carries the Vegvisir will never lose their way, even if the path is not known.

While not much is known about the Vegvisir and its usage amongst ancient Nordic peoples is debated the Vegvisir has become a popular symbol amongst people of Nordic faith and ancestry that represents finding ones way in life.

Triple Horn of Odin

The Triple Horn of Odin, also known as The Horn Triskelion, is a symbol representing wisdom and inspiration.

The dwarves Fjalar and Galar killed the wisest man in all the realms named Kvasir who is said to have known the answer to any question he might be asked. They took his blood and mixed it with honey to make a mead and placed it into 3 drinking horns.

Odin used his unmatched wit to convince the giantess princess Gunnlod to allow him to have 1 drink from each horn over a 3-day period. When taking his drinks, he managed to take the entire content of the horn into his mouth and on the 3rd day shape-shifted into an Eagle and returned to Asgard where he distributed the mead to whomever he saw fit.

The Nordic Triskelion is a symbol for artists, scholars, story tellers and tricksters representing wisdom, cleverness, guile and a quick tongue.

Mjolnir

Thor's Hammer, known as Mjollnir, is one of the most prolific symbols in Nordic history. Thor is the God of Thunder and protector of

Asgard and his hammer is the most powerful weapon in all the realms.

Mjollnir, pronounced "myarl-neer", was crafted by Dwarves and is a symbol of protection, consecration and blessings and has the power to banish Chaos from any entity. It is an important symbol in weddings, funerals and any other ceremony that involved the blessings of the Cosmos.

The Nordic peoples commonly wore a pendant around their necks representing Mjolnir and is found in many ancient Nordic burial sites. Mjolnir is one of, if not the most common Nordic symbols and can still be seen today worn by pagans around the world.

The Helm of Awe

The Helm of Awe is a symbol of power that has the ability to strike fear in the hearts of any who would oppose you. Eight Algiz Runes protrude form a central point creating a shield that exudes immeasurable strength.

In the Nordic Poetic Edda the dragon Fafnir attributes his power to The Helm of Awe and says "The Helm of Awe I wore before the sons of men, In defense of my treasure; Amongst all I alone was strong, I thought to myself, for I found no power a match to my own."

Ancient rituals would have practitioners of magick draw the rune between the brows and would imbue the wear the power of serpents to strike fear in the hearts of their opponents.

Gallery

I'm including the following gallery so you'll have a large image of each symbol in the book to trace or even cut out. One side of the page will have the image and the other side will be blank so you can add your own notes or write your own spells and rituals.

You can follow me on Instagram @BrittanyNightshadeOfficial and please give me a review on Amazon, I really appreciate the feedback.

Merry Met!
-Brittany Nightshade

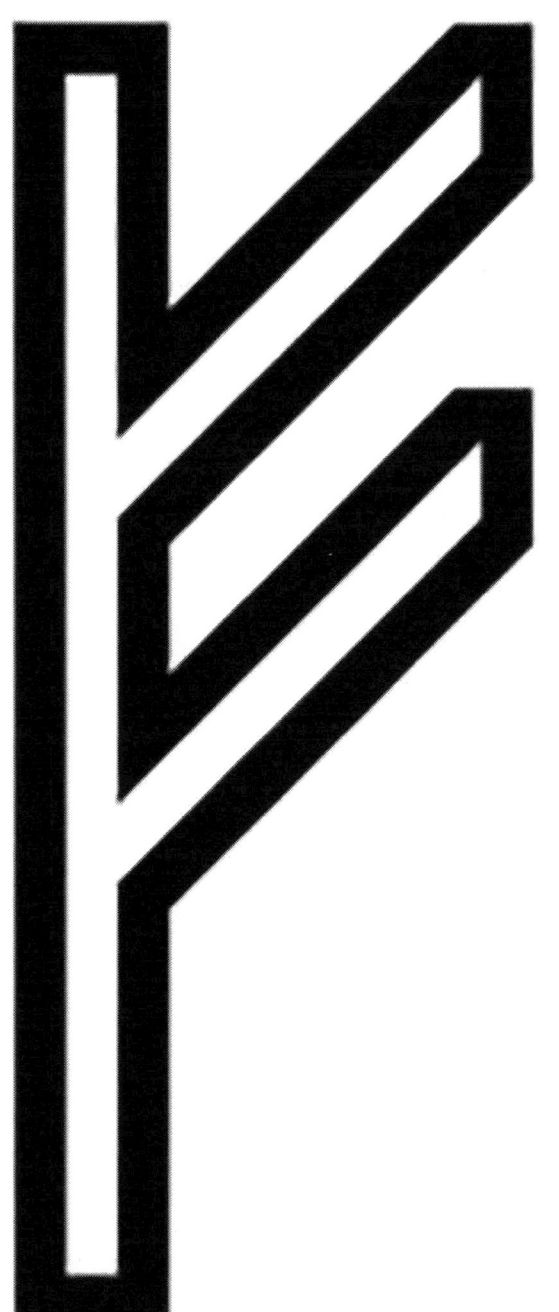

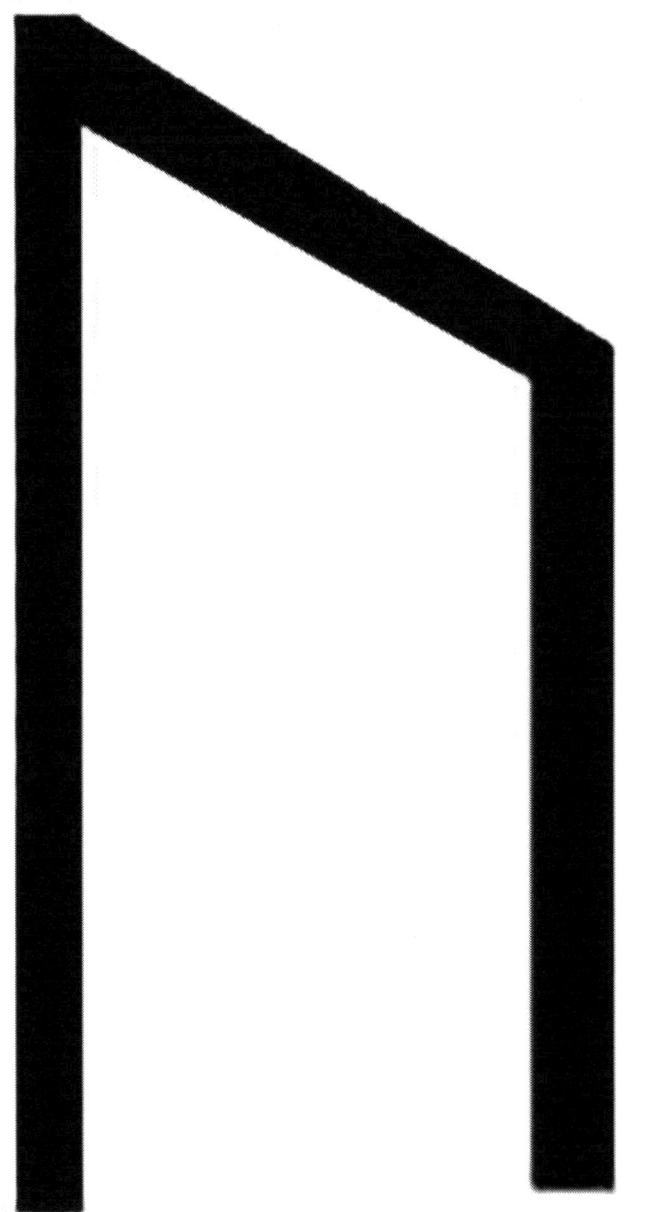

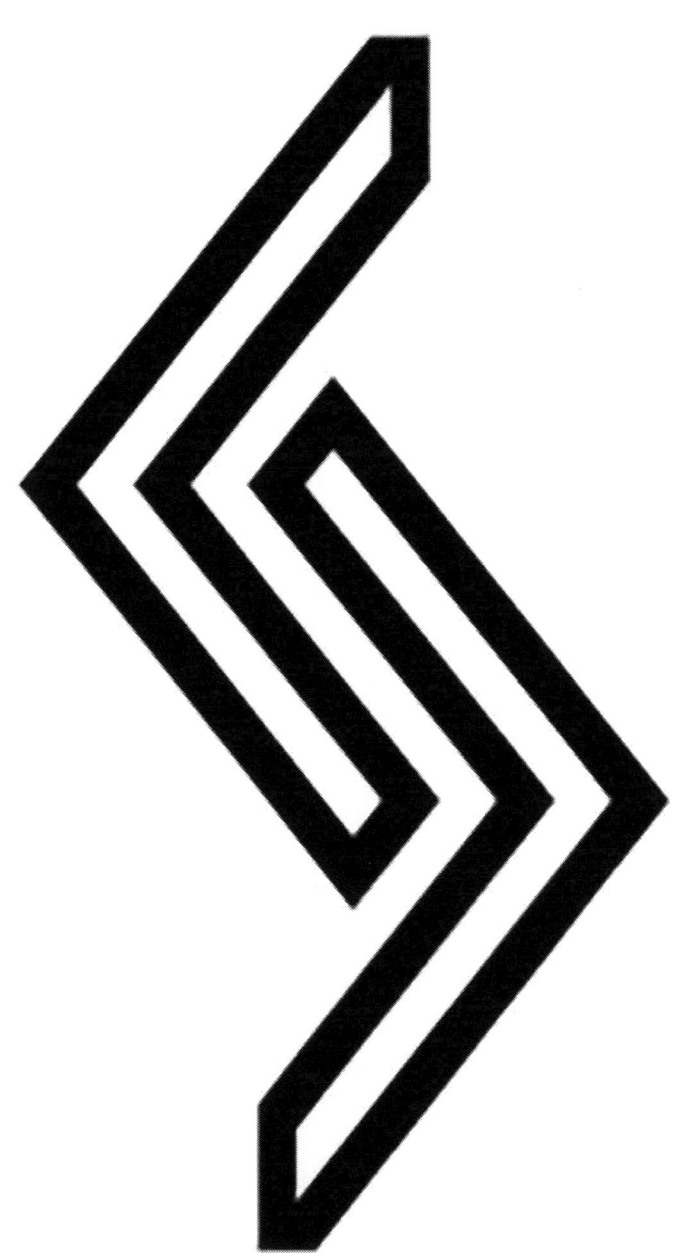

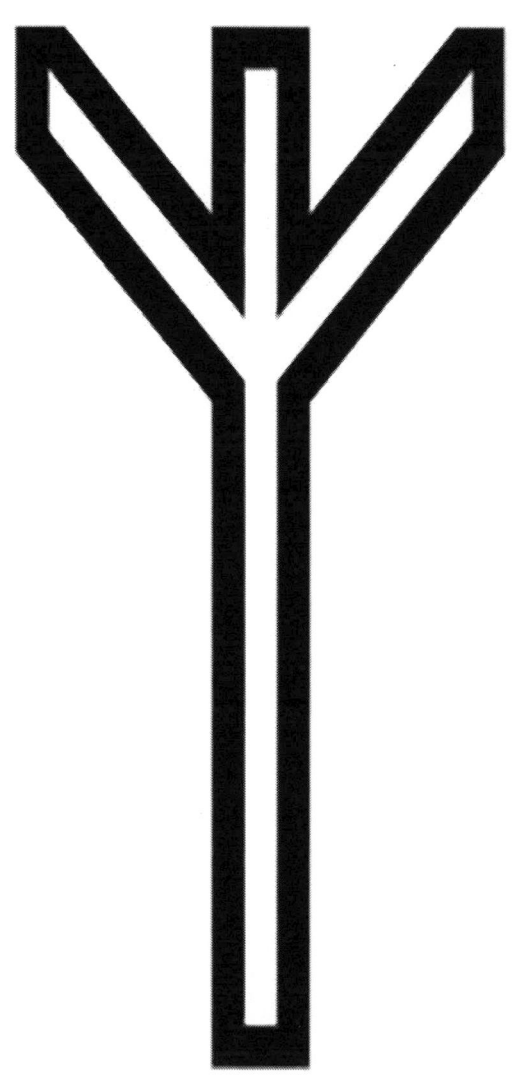

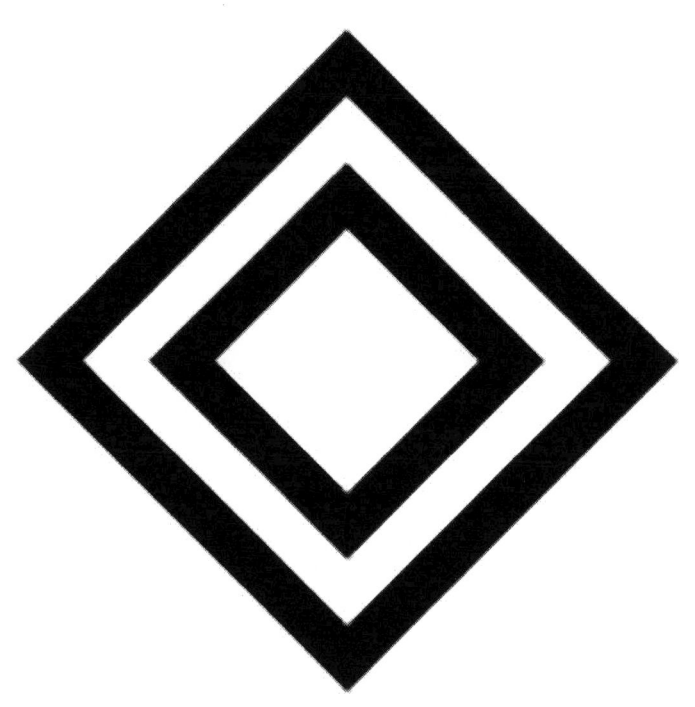

Printed in Great Britain
by Amazon